London's High Tea

I ate some amazing food during my weeklong adventure in London. I knew I would! I salivated right and left when I did my research before leaving. I always have an epic plan before I leave for any international trip – I research museums, events, markets, foods, and restaurants. Each trip, for me, is an opportunity to explore a new culture to inspire a new international dinner at Chez Nous Dinners.

London has everything, and no one discourages you from ordering a slice of cake with your cup of tea. I adore cake, and drink a heck of a lot of tea, so this was the place for me! I knew I wanted to have a proper High Tea during my travels. Historically, tea was a luxury item in European cities, imported from the East and only accessible for the Aristocracy. With the increase of steamboat and rail travel, tea became more attainable, but the cultural aspects of the elite "High Tea" remain. Did you know how the term "High Tea" came about? Generally, the aristocracy would take their tea reclined on lovely couches amidst their most wealthy companions, but High Tea would be taken at a proper table – literally, higher up!

I had High Tea at Cellarium Café in London. Cellarium cafe is a historic storage room of the monks at the abbey. The lovely vaulted space was whitewashed and repurposed into an airy cafe that offers a wide array of sandwiches and cakes and a delicious, while affordable, high tea! I was served a three tier stand of delicate little tea sandwiches, scones with butter and strawberry jam, and an array of tiny, single-serve cakes. I really enjoyed the meal and some of the flavors I had the opportunity to savor made their way to our menu for High Tea.

I put a great deal of preparation into the presentation and dishes. I wanted to serve several teas at a time, so I scoured Ebay for antique teapots to add to what I already had. I found a beautiful blue and 22 karat gold teapot and cup from Limoges, as well as a Silver Edwardian teapot from England. I paired this with my Lomonosov Royal Porcelain teapot from Russia to make a bit of a trifecta of the three biggest tea-drinking nations in Europe. I did not have any tiered platters, so I used some display goop to mount plates and cake stands together for that fancy tiered look.

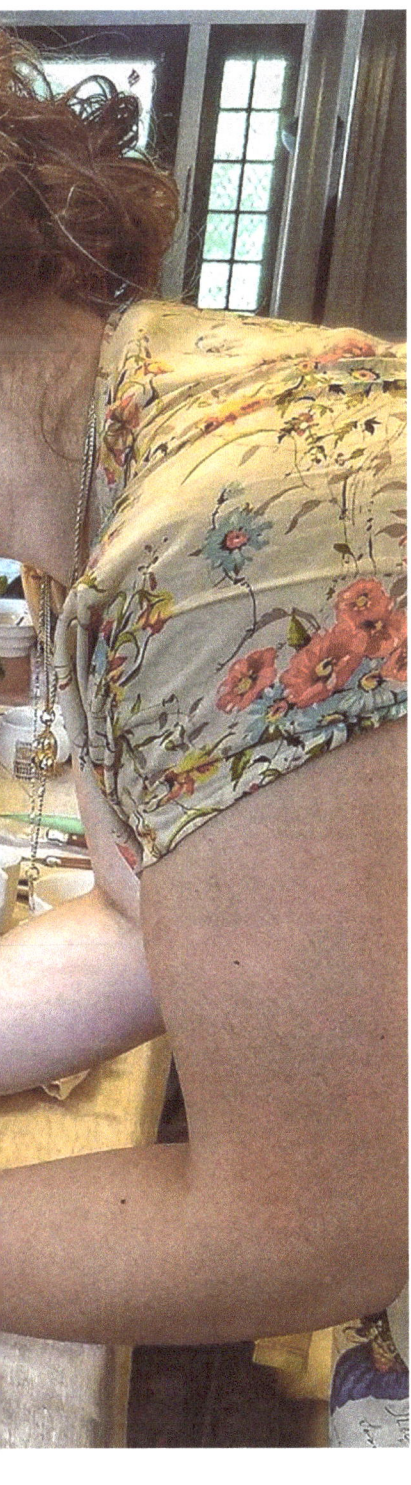

High Tea

To serve a high tea, I recommend 3-4 different teas. Serve 2 black teas, a green tea, and perhaps an herbal infusion. High tea can be served in courses, but it is much easier to present a table-scape of savories and sweets. A high tea has 3 requirements: tea sandwiches, scones, and cakes.

The Art of Tea   5

savories:

Tea Sandwiches   7
- Coronation Chicken
- Smoked Salmon and Dill
- Cucumber and Mint

Perfect Sandwich Bread   9

scones:

Sultana Scones   11
Butter and Clotted Cream   13
Jams   15
- Rhubarb, Strawberry, Mixed Berry, Mango

desserts:

Macaron   17
- Earl Grey with Lemon or Lavender Buttercream
- Lavender with Lemon Buttercream
- Chocolate with Orange Blossom Buttercream
- Matcha with Lemon or Matcha Buttercream

Victoria Sandwich Cake   21
Sachertorte   23

The Art of the Tea

Tea is the most commonly consumed drink in the world, and each country has their own tradition for serving tea. In Russia, a concentrated brew of tea is prepared in a small porcelain teapot and served with hot water from a samovar. We Russians love ours with lemon and a hunk of sugar. In Turkey, it is served in tall glasses with sugar. In North Africa, mint green tea is poured from silver tea pots lifted high in the air into beautiful colored glasses. The distance the tea travels builds a layer of froth in the glass. In India, tea is infused with a cinnamon and clove masala and paired with milk and sugar. Each culture has their own traditions, but today we explore the British tea tradition! Great Britain has created an incredible culture around tea, infusing their social hierarchy with the steeped leaves.

Tea originated in China around 2500 BC. By the 1600's, the Portuguese brought tea back to Europe and gave roots to a lasting tradition. By the 1650's tea came to England, and the tea mania truly began. Since then, tea has been at the center during the building of empires, businesses, controversy, and revolution.

Historically, access to tea has separated the different social classes, but today, it serves to bring people together. Everyone in Great Britain drinks tea, especially a hot cup of black tea with milk and sugar or a slice of lemon (never both!). Entire meals are organized around drinking a cup of tea. Those with time to spare stop for tea leisurely to gather with friends, while the hard workers of the land take a mid-afternoon break to drink tea and a biscuit. Most famously, the British take their tea with finger sandwiches and an array of tea cakes. This is what has come to be known as High Tea.

Some hints on making tea:

1. Buy the best quality tea that you can. I prefer full leaf tea to tea bags. When you buy tea bags, you are frequently purchasing the dust and leftovers of the tea leaf.
2. Use fresh water. Do not re-boil tea water, as this releases the oxygen and makes it less fresh.
3. Boil your water to the right temperature. Black teas require a boil of 212°F (100°C) while green tea needs to only be brewed to 175°F (80°C) .
4. Have the right tea to water ratio. You want 1 teaspoon of tea leaves and 1 ¼ cup (300 mL) of hot water per person.
5. Brew for the right amount of time, then remove the tea leaves. Three to four minutes is the golden rule!
6. Run the tea pot under hot water to warm it before adding tea.

Trifecta of Tea Sandwiches: Cucumber Mint, Smoked Salmon, and Coronation Chicken

makes 16 finger sandwiches each

I had a friend who once told me his ex-girlfriend would never order sandwiches at a restaurant because if she pays for food, she demands more than someone just stacking ingredients between two pieces of bread. I can see the logic, but man, I love sandwiches! I order sandwiches all the time! There is an art to the sandwich however, and for High Tea, I didn't want to just stack ingredients between two pieces of bread. I have a few friends that are either vegetarian or pescatarian, and one who refuses to eat fish, so I wanted to create something that would suit all.

coronation chicken:

1. Heat oil in a large pan and toast the curry powder and turmeric for about a minute.
2. Add in the broken up chicken and mix to coat. Remove from heat.
3. Transfer to a large mixing bowl. Add the remaining ingredients. Mix, and season with salt and pepper to taste.
4. Butter both sides of bread and divide filling between the sandwiches.
5. Cut off crusts and slice each sandwich into four finger sandwiches.

smoked salmon:

1. Mix mayonnaise, capers, gherkins, parsley, chives, and lemon together.
   Season with salt and pepper to taste.
2. Butter both sides of bread.
   Spread half with the tartar mixture.
   Divide salmon between the sandwiches.
3. Cut off crusts and slice each sandwich into four finger sandwiches.

cucumber mint:

1. Trim cucumber to the length of your bread and slice thinly, lengthwise.
   Spread out cucumbers on several plates and sprinkle with salt. Leave for 20 minutes.
   Pat cucumbers dry on both sides.
2. Beat together cream cheese, mint, lemon juice, and zest. Season with salt and pepper to taste.
   Butter both sides of bread.
3. Divide cream cheese mixture between all slices of bread.
   Carefully place about 3 slices of cucumber on one side of bread.
   Sandwich with the second prepared slice.
4. Cut off crusts and slice each sandwich into four finger sandwiches.

coronation chicken:

1 tablespoon olive oil
4 1/5 teaspoons curry Madras
1 teaspoon turmeric
3 boiled chicken breasts, sliced thinly and then broken up
4-5 tablespoons mayonnaise
2 tablespoons mango jam
1 tablespoon golden raisins, chopped coarsely
2 tablespoons dried apricots, chopped coarsely
2 tablespoons chopped cilantro
salt and pepper to taste
butter, to spread
8 slices of white bread

smoked salmon:

scant 1/2 cup (100 mL) mayonnaise
2 tablespoons capers, chopped
2 tablespoons gherkins, chopped
1 tablespoon chopped parsley
1 tablespoon chopped chives
1 tablespoon lemon juice
1 teaspoon lemon zest
salt and pepper to taste
4 ounces (115 g) smoked salmon
butter, to spread
8 slices of rye bread

cucumber mint:

1 English cucumber
8 ounces (225 g) cream cheese
2 tablespoons mint, chopped
zest of 1 lemon
juice of 1/2 lemon
salt and pepper to taste
butter, to spread
8 slices of white bread

Perfect Sandwich Bread

makes 2 loaves

1. Whisk and dissolve yeast in the milk. Add to bowl of stand mixer with kneading attachment.
2. Add the sugar, salt, and beaten eggs.
   Add 1 cup (120 g) flour. Mix on low until incorporated.
   Add 3 tablespoons butter and 2 more cups (240 g) flour. Mix on low speed until incorporated.
   Add remaining flour and mix on low speed until gathered into a ball.
3. Mix on medium speed for about 10 minutes until smooth and pliable.
4. Cover in oil and place in a covered bowl. Place in cold oven with pilot light on and allow to rise to twice its size. Depending on the temperature, it may take between 1 and 2 hours.
5. Flour a counter and knead the loaf for 3 minutes.
   Add a bit more oil if needed when returning to bowl. Rise for 45 more minutes.
6. Meanwhile, coat the inside or two 5x9 inch (13x23 cm) baking tins using about 1 tablespoon butter per pan.
7. Flatten the dough and divide in half.
   Fold into a rectangle with folded sides down and place in the tins.
   Cover and let rise until just taller than the rim, about 45 minutes to 1 hour.
8. Preheat oven to 400°F (205°C) with convection fan on, or 25°F (15°C) higher without.
9. Melt remaining butter and brush onto tops of loaves.
   Bake for 10 minutes.
   Lower heat to 350°F (180°C) and bake for another 20 minutes.

The first step in making a beautiful sandwich, of course, is the bread! Modifying some of my sweet breads and challah recipes, I found what I think is a perfect loaf of white sandwich bread. It has a bit of sweetness to make either a sweet or savory sandwich and a soft, but golden brown crust achieved by a thin coat of butter before baking. This loaf is hard to mess up and lasts at least 3 days wrapped on the counter. I have not had the chance to see if it will last longer because it keeps disappearing!

---

1 1/2 cup (360 mL) warm milk

2 1/4 teaspoons yeast

1/4 cup (50 g) sugar

2 1/2–3 teaspoons salt

6 tablespoons unsalted butter, separated, softened

2 eggs, beaten

5 1/2 cups (660 g) bread flour

Sultana Scones

makes 16-18 scones

These scones are not the hard triangles we are accustomed to in coffee houses. I use White Lily light all-purpose flour for these. The flour is milled very finely which, when mixed with butter, creates a beautiful light scone that melts in your mouth. Allowing the dough to rest for two sessions also helps maintain an even texture and relaxed gluten in the dough. We served these for our High Tea party with great success, I did not have any leftovers and had to make my own breakfast the next morning! These pair beautifully with a variety of jams.

3 cups (360 g) + 2 tablespoons White Lily flour, or fine pastry flour
5 teaspoons baking powder
1/2 teaspoon salt
8 tablespoons unsalted butter, cut into small pieces, cold
scant 1/2 cup (90 g) sugar
1/2 cup (75 g) sultanas (golden raisins)
3/4 cup (180 g) milk
1 egg, beaten – for glaze

1. Combine flour, baking powder, and salt in a large bowl.
2. Mix butter in with your fingers until it looks like bread crumbs.
   Add sugar, mix in.
   Add sultanas (raisins), mix in.
3. Add milk, pouring it over the surface not just in one spot. Stir, careful not to over-stir. You should still see small bits of butter.
   Cover and rest for 30 minutes.
4. On a floured surface, roll out to 1/2 to 3/4 inch (1.25-2 cm) thick.
5. Cut into 2 1/2 inch (6.35 cm) rounds. Re-roll dough if needed.
6. Place scones on parchment lined cookie sheet and brush with egg.
   Cover and rest 30 more minutes.
7. Preheat oven to 350°F (180°C).
   Bake 12-15 minutes until golden.
8. Store wrapped in plastic for 1-2 days. Freeze for longer storage.

Butter and Clotted Cream

serves 12-16

clotted cream:

1. Make sure you buy pasteurized heavy cream. Ultra-pasteurized does not work as well.
   Place heavy cream in a Dutch oven or pot/pan with a large surface area. Your goal is to have 1 inch (2.5 cm) of cream in a pot. Cover with aluminum foil.
2. Bake at 180°F (80°C) for at least 8 hours but up to 12 hours.
3. Cool and place in the fridge for another 8 hours, perhaps while you are at work!
4. Carefully separate the thick layer at the top (the clotted cream) from the rest of the cream. Store for a few days in the refrigerator. Use the rest of the cream to cook with.

butter and buttermilk:

1. Dump heavy cream into stand mixer. Beat as you would whipped cream. However, instead of whipping, the cream will eventually separate.
2. Drain out the buttermilk and reserve for baking.
   Continue draining the butter for a few hours, moving it around with a spoon to get as much buttermilk out as possible.
3. Mix in a bit of salt for flavor and store in a container that seals.
   Lasts refrigerated for at least two weeks.

Clotted cream is not something you come across frequently in America. I have only been served this amazing juncture between whipped cream and butter once, during High Tea at an Alice in Wonderland themed tea room in New York. Clotted cream is delicious, but rather pricey! Luckily for us all, it is incredibly easy to make!

One time in high school, I accidentally made butter. I was trying to make whipped cream but left the cream out on the counter for too long before whipping it. I realized that what I had was butter. Since then, I have been doing it on purpose!

---

clotted cream:

6 cups (720 mL) pasteurized heavy cream

butter and buttermilk:

4 cups (480 mL) heavy cream at room temperature
freshly ground salt, to taste

Jams

makes between 4-8 cups each

rhubarb jam:
1. Mix all ingredients in a large Dutch Oven and cook for 40 minutes, stirring occasionally.
2. Once slightly reduced, and the rhubarb turns into a viscous mash, turn off heat.
3. To process, boil clean jars and lids, or place in the oven at 180°F (80°C) for 20 minutes. Place on a towel of some sort or a wooden counter, not a cold stone or metal one.
4. Carefully pour jam into glass containers, leaving about a half an inch (1 cm) of room. Clean the rim and cover with lids.
5. Place in large pot and cover with hot water. Do not use cold water as jars will explode. Make sure enough water covers the jars that lids remain covered for 15 minute boil.
6. Boil for 15 minutes. Allow to cool, remove from water, and label jars for storage. Refrigerate once opened, but otherwise they should store for at least a year.

strawberry jam and mixed berry jam:
1. Combine all ingredients in a large Dutch oven and cook for about 20 minutes until thickened. Stir occasionally.
2. Take a teaspoon full and place on a plate in freezer for 2 minutes. Check if thick enough.
3. Process as above (steps 3-6).

mango jam with cardamom and saffron:
1. Combine mango, sugar, water, and rum in a Dutch oven. Simmer for 30 minutes or so. The syrup should start to become a bit stringy and the mango pieces should fall apart if pressed against the side of the pot.
2. Turn off heat. Blend to desired consistency. Add saffron and cardamom and simmer another 3 minutes.
3. Process as above (steps 3-6).

Jam has always been a part of my life. When I was a kid, we spent the summers in a little cottage in the woods. I would spend my days wandering about picking raspberries, blueberries, and strawberries in the woods to make jams.

———

rhubarb jam:
3 1/2 pounds (1.5 kg) rhubarb, chopped
2 3/4 cups (550 g) sugar
zest of one lemon
1/2 cup (120 mL) orange juice
2/3 cup (180 mL) water

strawberry or mixed berry jam:
2 pounds (900 g) strawberries, fresh or frozen, chopped in half (or 2 pounds mixed berry)
4 cups (800 g) sugar
zest of one lemon
1/4 cup sugar

mango jam with cardamom:
6 mangoes, peeled, seeded, and chopped to 1 inch (2.5 cm)
4 1/2 cups (900 g) sugar
1 cup (240 mL) water
1 cup (240 mL) dark rum
1/2 teaspoon cardamom
pinch of saffron

Macaron

makes 60-80 cookies

The French Macaron has a cult following now-a-days! It didn't when I first fell in love with them in New York 12 years ago, but for some reason, people still call them Macaroons. Go figure! Due to the famed difficulty of properly preparing these cookies, French pastry chefs would (and still do!) display them in their windows to show off their talent. See, a Macaron is not a Macaron without "Le pied" or the foot. Le pied is that fuzzy bit at the base of each cookie where the dough seems like it is escaping the beautiful dome above. That is exactly what is happening. The cookies are piped onto parchment and left for 10 minutes to form a crust. As the cookie bakes, the air expands and pushes some almond dough out to create the foot. When I first started making these 10 years ago, I read that you must smack the cookie sheet against the counter before letting the crust form. I have, without question, been following this advice and will require you to do the same!

The one thing I don't love about this delicious almond pastry is all of the food coloring that goes into making those beautiful displays! For the most part, the different flavors come from the filling, but the shells themselves are generally just food coloring. I try to avoid food coloring, so I have been doing crazy experiments with alternative ways to flavor and color the Macaron. Let me tell you, adding raspberry jam does not work! Do not add any liquid to your meringue; bad things happen. However, dry flavors like ground lavender, rosemary, rose petal, matcha, or Earl Grey tea do wonders!

Make them a day ahead and store in the fridge between layers of parchment to let the flavors blend. You can store them for at least 3 days in the fridge.

continued next page.

The following page will guide you in creating these delicious flavor combinations, or use them as a guide to create your own pairing!

_____

Earl Grey Macaron with Lemon Buttercream

Earl Grey Macaron with Lavender Buttercream

Lavender Macaron with Lemon Buttercream

Chocolate Macaron with Orange Blossom Buttercream

Matcha Macaron with Matcha Buttercream

Matcha Macaron with Lemon Buttercream

macaron:

1. Preheat oven to 325°F (165°C).
2. Line 3 cookie sheets with parchment (or measure 3 sheets of parchment for your cookie sheet). Using a pencil, draw 1 1/4 inch (3 cm) rounds 1 inch (2.5 cm) apart on your cookie sheet. I used the smallest of my biscuit rounds as a tool, but bottle caps work too. You need about 160 rounds.
3. Mix confectioners sugar, almonds, and tea leaves (or lavender, matcha, or cocoa) together and grind in a food processor until smooth. If chunks are formed, break them apart with your fingers in a bowl.
4. Whisk egg whites with a pinch of salt and cream of tartar until soft peaks form.
5. Carefully add the sugar and whisk until smooth and shiny.
   Fold half of the almond mixture into the meringue.
   Carefully fold the second half into the meringue.
6. Fill pastry bag with thickest round piping attachment. Pipe into drawn circles, one cookie sheet at a time.
7. Whack the cookie sheet against the counter and leave uncovered for 10 minutes to allow a shell to form. Do not skip this step!
8. Bake for 15 minutes and slide off of cookie sheet onto cooling rack.
9. To assemble, sandwich about 1/4-1/2 teaspoon buttercream between each set of shells. Store in an airtight container between layers of parchment in the fridge. Bring out at least an hour before serving.

buttercream:

1. If using lavender flowers, grind with the sugar in a food processor.
2. Beat butter, sugar, and any other flavors.

macaron:

3 cups (375 g) confectioners sugar
2 2/3 cups (280 g) ground almond
6 large egg whites
Pinch of salt
Pinch of cream of tartar
3/4 cup (150 g) granulated sugar

for Earl Grey macaron:

4 tablespoons Earl Grey tea

for lavender macaron:

4 tablespoons lavender flowers

for matcha macaron:

2 teaspoons matcha powder

for chocolate macaron:

4 tablespoons cocoa powder
remove 4 tablespoons confectioner's sugar

---

basic buttercream:

8 tablespoons unsalted butter
2/3 cup (85 g) confectioners sugar

for lavender buttercream:

1 1/2 teaspoon dried lavender flowers

for lemon buttercream:

zest of one lemon
juice of 1/4 lemon or a few drops of lemon extract

for matcha buttercream:

1 teaspoon matcha

for orange blossom buttercream:

2-3 drops orange blossom water

Victoria Sandwich Cake

serves 9-12

This might just be the most British cake that we served at High Tea. The cake became a popular tea-time treat during the reign of Queen Victoria. It is said that it was her favorite cake! Traditionally, this delicious, buttery, sponge cake is served with raspberry jam and whipped cream sandwiched in between two cakes. We decided to go with raspberry jam and fresh strawberries since they were in season.

1. Preheat oven to 350°F (180°C).
2. Cream butter and sugar. Add eggs, one at a time. Whisk in. Add baking powder and 1 cup (120 g) flour. Whisk in. Add remaining flour. Whisk in.
3. Grease two 8 inch (20 cm) spring form pans. Cover bottoms in aluminum foil or place on a cookie sheet with raised edges.
4. Divide the dough between pans. Bake for 20-30 minutes until golden brown.
5. Meanwhile, whip heavy cream until soft peaks form.
6. Remove from oven and leave in tins for about 15 minutes. Then remove from tins and cool completely on a cooling rack.
7. Once cooled, place one cake on a serving platter.
8. Spread half of the jam on top. Pipe whipped cream all over the cake surface, careful to make the edges look nice.
Arrange strawberries on top. Place second cake on top and dust with confectioner's sugar.

cake:

scant 2 cups (230 g) cake flour

3 1/4 teaspoons baking powder

16 tablespoons unsalted butter, softened

1 cup (200 g) sugar

4 large eggs, beaten

filling:

1/2 cup Rhubarb Jam, p. 15

1 cup (240 mL) heavy cream

8 ounces (225 g) fresh strawberries, sliced

garnish:

confectioner's sugar for dusting

Sachertorte

serves 10-12

1. For the cake, first melt the chocolate. If you have a double boiler, that is the ideal method. But I generally put it all in a microwave safe bowl with 8 tablespoons of butter cut up and microwave for 45 seconds. Mix softened butter and chocolate together, and microwave for another 45 seconds.
2. Meanwhile, cream the remaining butter with 1 cup (200 g) of sugar.
   Beat in the egg yolks, 1 at a time.
3. Carefully mix in the melted chocolate.
   Add half of the flour as well as all of the ground almond flour.
4. Separately, whip egg whites with a pinch of salt or cream of tartar until soft peaks form. Add 1/2 cup (100 g) of sugar and whisk until smooth and glossy with firm peaks.
5. Stir 1/4 of the egg whites into the chocolate mixture.
6. Add the remaining flours.
7. Fold in the remaining egg whites.
8. Preheat oven to 325°F (165°C).
9. Butter or oil two 8 inch (20 cm) round spring form cake tins, cover bottoms in foil.
10. Pour in batter and level tops.
11. Bake for 30-40 minutes until set.
12. Leave in tins for 10 minutes to cool, then remove to cooling rack to cool completely before use.
13. Meanwhile, bring rum and jam to a boil in a small saucepan. Cook for 2-3 minutes until combined and push through a sieve to separate out any chunks. Cool completely!
14. Cut off any bump that may have grown during baking. You want a perfectly flat cake.
15. Place one cake on serving platter.
    Top with 1/2 of apricot jam.
    Add second layer making sure it is even.

continued next page.

Sachertorte is quite the legend! It is Vienna's most popular dessert! It starts off as a chocolate sponge cake lightened with 8 egg whites. Two cakes are sandwiched with apricot jam with a touch of rum and a chocolate glaze encases the whole cake! It is generally served with whipped cream.

---

cake:

2 cups (240 g) pastry flour

1/2 cup (60 g) almond flour

4 tablespoons cocoa powder

10 ounce (285 g) bag of dark chocolate chips (honestly, 9oz, I always eat a bit as I am cooking)

18 tablespoons unsalted butter

1 1/2 cup (300 g) sugar, separated

10 egg yolks

8 egg whites

apricot jam:

1 1/2 cup apricot jam

3 tablespoons dark rum

1 packet unflavored gelatin

chocolate glaze:

1/2 cup (120 mL)
   + 1 tablespoon heavy cream

1 cup (200 g)
   + 2 tablespoons sugar

2/3 cup (70 g) cocoa powder

16. Cover the whole cake with a thin layer of apricot. You may have some extra; don't force it on as that will make putting the chocolate glaze on tougher. Instead, save it and eat it with those bits of cake you just trimmed!
17. To make the glaze, sprinkle gelatin over the heavy cream in a small pot. Let it absorb for a minute.
18. Whisk in the sugar and cocoa, and simmer on medium-low heat, continuously stirring for about 8 minutes or so. It will bubble and become shiny and thick.
19. Cool for a bit. If you cool it all the way, it will set a bit too much; just warm it up for a few seconds while whisking.
20. Pour about half on top of the cake. Using a flat frosting spatula, turn your cake slowly while keeping your wrist in the same position and gently level out the top while forcing some frosting down the sides. (really invest in this spatula if you like cakes; much better than any knife!)
21. Continue spinning the cake while adding a bit of glaze at a time to the sides of your cake. The trick is to move the cake, not your arm. Maybe invest in a spinning cake stand as well. I wish I had one!
22. Let the glaze set; it will develop a bit of a crust. You can decorate it at that point if you like! I added a thin trail of ground almonds and lavender flowers.

www.ingramcontent.com/pod-product-compliance
Lightning Source LLC
Chambersburg PA
CBHW061937290426
44113CB00025B/2944